But Is It Art?

Urban Street Art

Alix Wood

Gareth Stevens
PUBLISHING

Please visit our website, **www.garethstevens.com**. For a free color catalog of all our high-quality books, call toll free 1-800-542-2595 or fax 1-877-542-2596.

Library of Congress Cataloging-in-Publication Data

Wood, Alix.
 Urban street art / Alix Wood.
    pages cm. — (But is it art?)
 Includes index.
ISBN 978-1-4824-2295-5 (pbk.)
ISBN 978-1-4824-2296-2 (6 pack)
ISBN 978-1-4824-2293-1 (library binding)
1. Art and popular culture—Juvenile literature. 2. Street art—Juvenile literature.
3. Outdoor art—Juvenile literature. 4. Offenses against property—Juvenile literature. I. Title.
 N72.S6W66 2015
 709.173'2—dc23

2014033435

First Edition

Published in 2015 by
Gareth Stevens Publishing
111 East 14th Street, Suite 349
New York, NY 10003

© Alix Wood Books

Produced for Gareth Stevens by Alix Wood Books
Designed by Alix Wood
Editor: Eloise Macgregor

Photo credits:
Cover © Joanbanjo; 1, 10, 18 © Neale Cousland/Shutterstock; 4 © Jean-Luc Henry; 5 © Alvaro León; 6 © Shyguy24x7; 7 © An-d; 8 © LuigiNovi /Wikimedia Commons; 9 top © Staggerbear; 9 bottom © www.brandalism.org.uk; 11 top © digitalarti.com; 11 bottom © Graffiti Research Lab; 12 public domain; 13 © Pinkyjosef; 14 © Ou812; 15 © Sarah Gilbert; 16 top, 26 right © Shutterstock; 16 bottom © mandritoiu/Shutterstock; 17 top © Richard Thornton/Shutterstock; 17 bottom © hans engbers/Shutterstock; 19 top © Prokura; 19 bottom © Kencf0618; 20 © meunierd/Shutterstock; 21 top © Andaje; 21 middle © theinfo; 21 bottom © Rich Anderson; 22 top © grahamc99; 22 bottom, 23 © Salim Fadhley; 24 © Disdero; 25 top © Heather Hall; 25 bottom © A.Savin; 26 left © Jean-Luc Henry; 27 top © mike castle; 27 bottom © Mark Holsworth; 29 © Bukk

Printed in the United States of America
CPSIA compliance information: Batch # CW15GS: For further information contact Gareth Stevens, New York, New York at 1-800-542-2595.

Contents

What Is Urban Street Art? 4

Yarn Bombing.............................. 6

Subvertising 8

Light-Up Street Art.........................10

Why Create Street Art?......................12

Lock On Street Sculptures 14

Sidewalk Art 16

Wheatpasting.............................18

Sticker Bombing 20

Ben Wilson, Gum Artist! 22

Lovelocks 24

Guerrilla Gardening..........................26

Is Urban Street Art Art?.....................28

Glossary.................................30

For More Information 31

Index 32

What Is Urban Street Art?

Urban street art is art created in public areas. An "urban area" means a town or city. Urban street art is often made for free, by people who want their art to be seen by many people. Sometimes the artists have a message that they want people to see. Other street artists simply want to make the city or town look more fun and colorful.

There are many different types of urban street art. The artists all have the same aim, though. They want to bring art into our streets. They don't always have the permission of the people who own or manage the land, though, which can lead to problems.

Arty Fact

The term "urban street art" can include **graffiti**. Graffiti is writing or drawing on walls. Urban street art is usually used to describe other street art besides graffiti, though.

Some urban gardeners plant flowers or vegetables in ugly areas of rough land. If they do not have permission to do this, it can be seen as breaking the law.

There are many different definitions of what people think art is. Which of these do you agree with?

Art is:

- anything that an artist calls art
- something that is created with imagination and skill. It must be either beautiful, or express important ideas or feelings
- a mixture of "form" (the way something is created) and "content" (the "what" that has been created)

WHAT DO YOU THINK?

Is planting flowers in an old toilet art? It would not have taken much skill. The artist did use their imagination to think of using the toilet as a flowerpot, however. The artist created something more beautiful than a dump site, too.

"Yarn bombers" decorated these street posts with knitting!

Yarn Bombing

Yarn bombing, or guerrilla knitting as it is sometimes called, is a type of street art using knitted or crocheted yarn. Unlike some other street art, it can be easily removed.

Yarn bombing is believed to have started in Texas. Knitters there wanted to find a use for leftover yarn and unfinished projects. The idea has spread worldwide. Groups of knitters often prepare works together. The most popular form is the "cozy." A cozy is a knitted cover that is sewn around an object.

WHAT DO YOU THINK?

Do you think anyone could object to yarn bombing? It usually makes people smile. In bad weather the yarn can get rotten and lose its color. It is easy to take down, though.

A yarn-bombed bicycle in Sweden!

Yarn bombing is the art of making a public place or object more attractive by covering it in knitting. It is fun as it is so colorful and unexpected.

Yarn bombing turns everyday objects into art. It can bring color to a drab area and make people laugh and talk to each other.

Arty Fact

Knit the City is a yarn-bombing group from London, UK. They create large pieces. They once made a big spider web, complete with spider and victims! They prefer the word "yarnstorming" to describe what they do.

Subvertising

Subvertising is making fake **advertisements** which fool people into thinking they are real. After a double take, people realize their mistake. Subvertising often contains a comment on the product that you mistakenly believe the poster is advertising.

One of Ron English's clever subvertising posters warns against the high sugar corn syrup used in kids' breakfast cereal.

Ron English is a street artist who specializes in subvertising. His billboard poster designs have been critical of everything from the high sugar content in children's breakfast cereals to cigarette advertising. He has even placed empty cereal packets covered with his art onto grocery stores' shelves, to help inform shoppers about high sugar!

Ron English

WHAT DO YOU THINK?

Every day we see advertisements trying to get us to buy things. Because advertisers want to sell to us, they will only tell us what is good about a product. Do you think it is good for street artists to tell us what might be bad about a product, too?

During the 2008 Presidential election, Ron English merged the features of Barack Obama and Abraham Lincoln to make "Abraham Obama." Prints were sold to raise funds and promote the Obama campaign. "Abraham Obama" street murals were created in several cities, too.

There are some organized subvertising events around the world. An event in the UK known as "Brandalism" encourages artists to take over advertising spaces to get their own messages across.

Arty Fact

Subvertising is also called culture jamming. Radio jammers disrupt radio communications by sending out other signals on the same **wavelength**. Culture jammers disrupt the effect an advertisement has by using a similar looking advertisement with a different message.

"Ad nauseum" means a thing has been done over and over until it makes you feel ill. This clever Brandalism poster links too much **consumerism** with making you feel sick!

Light-Up Street Art

Some street artists use **projectors** and **LEDs** to create stunning light-up art. Artists can create displays that don't damage the surface they are on, and are simple to remove.

Several cities around the world have nighttime art festivals. Melbourne, Australia hosts a festival called White Nights. Artists create incredible light shows and **installations** for the festival.

LED throwies are small LED lights attached to a magnet. The magnet sticks to most metal surfaces.

Colorful images are projected onto buildings during Melbourne's White Nights festival.

Usually electricity and water together are dangerous. French artist Antonin Fourneau has created a safe LED wall out of thousands of LEDs. The bulbs light up if they are touched with water. You can use a wet paintbrush, a water spray, or even wet fingers to sketch a message or a drawing!

Some graffiti artists use **laser** lights to create street art. The message on the bridge pictured above is created with lasers. It is very important to only direct the light beam toward an area where there are no people or animals. Laser light can damage eyes.

WHAT DO YOU THINK?

Can something be art if it is not permanent? You can't keep or buy a light show. Only photographs or video remain once the display is over. A lot of street art just happens in the moment and then is gone. Can that be art?

Why Create Street Art?

Only some artists taking part in organized events actually get paid for it. Most artists create street art for the love of it. What drives artists to want to make public works of art?

Artists who create street art often work in studios, too. They create work in the street because they like the freedom it gives them. They can often create much larger pieces than they can in a studio. Their art can be seen by a wider audience, too. Many people don't go to galleries. The only way an artist can reach all kinds of people is to move out of the gallery and into a public space.

WHAT DO YOU THINK?

If art expresses important ideas or emotions, why the artist does it must be important. Is it necessary to know why someone creates an artwork to decide whether it is art or not?

This mural is by the famous street artist Banksy. Why did he create this? The cave painting reminds us just how old drawing on walls is! The man cleaning the wall is gently poking fun at society's desire to wipe art off the streets.

Many types of street art are illegal, and artists risk being arrested if they are caught. Because of this, many artists are **anonymous**. They may be in trouble if they are recognized. That makes it hard to become well-known for your work! Although the street artist known as Banksy is famous, no one actually knows who he is.

Some artists are driven by a need to get a **political** message across. Street artist Shepard Fairey believes all street art is political, because creating street art itself is a kind of protest.

One of the main driving forces for some types of street art is a desire to brighten up people's worlds. Making a funny wooly hat for a post isn't a strong political statement. It just brings a smile to people's faces.

Lock On Street Sculptures

Lock on street artists create sculptures which they chain or padlock onto objects such as lampposts or fences. The sculptures are often made to look like they are interacting with the object they are attached to.

Danish artist Tejn is considered the "founder" of lock on street art. He welds scrap metal together to make the sculptures, which he then "returns to the street" as art. Most of his welded iron sculptures are in Copenhagen, Denmark, and Berlin, Germany.

Two lock on sculptures by the street artist known as Tejn.

In Portland, Oregon, street artist Scott Wayne Indiana chained a toy horse to an old metal ring that used to be used for tethering real horses. Since then, local people have joined the "horse project." Tiny plastic horses are now tied to rings all over the city. People leave hay and water, and even lassoes, saddles, and blankets for the horses, too!

When asked why he did it, Indiana explained that he loved the rings, and felt that people just weren't noticing them. He wanted to shake people out of their routines and get them to notice their surroundings.

WHAT DO YOU THINK?

The Portland horses have become a tourist attraction! Can you think of any reason why the horses might be a bad idea? Why do you think many local authorities do not want lock ons in their city? Could they be dangerous in any way?

Arty Fact

In many countries people chain white painted bicycles, sometimes called ghost bikes, to lampposts near where a cyclist has been killed. This acts as a memorial, and a reminder to drivers to take care near cyclists.

Sidewalk Art

Street artists create amazing sidewalk art using chalk. The art washes away in the rain and doesn't do permanent damage. Street artists can earn money with donations from passersby. Large companies sometimes employ street artists to create advertisements on busy streets and in shopping malls, too.

Some sidewalk artist groups hold street festivals and competitions. The best pavements are smooth, even surfaces, without many joins between the bricks. Street artists like working outside in a busy environment. Most will take photographs before their work washes away. They think of the photograph as being the end result of their work, so they don't get upset when the rain comes!

Arty Fact

Street painting was popular in 16th-century Italy. The artists were called "Madonnari" because they often drew the **Madonna** and child.

This sidewalk artist is reproducing Jan Vermeer's painting *Girl with a Pearl Earring*. Some passersby have put money into her shoebox.

Try making some sidewalk art yourself. Ask permission first before you start drawing on any paving. Use chalks to create your masterpiece. It's a good idea to practice your design on paper. Then lightly sketch the outline on the paving first to check it looks good from above. Pavement art sometimes has to be **distorted** to look best to passersby.

Street paintings that create an **optical illusion** like this one are best viewed from one angle. This art would not look as convincing if you looked at it from the other side. Some artists mark out the distorted shape they need to draw using a rope. They stand at the chosen viewpoint and adjust the rope until the shape looks right. Then they start drawing.

wheatpasting

Wheatpasting street art is created by artists drawing onto paper and then pasting the paper onto a wall. The posters can be difficult to remove. Wheatpasting is **illegal** unless artists have permission to paste in an area. There are special poster walls in some cities for wheatpasters to use.

All kinds of artwork can be done on wheatpaste posters. Street art like in the photograph below would be created in sections in a **studio**. It would then be brought to the wall and pasted up. Wheatpasting gives street artists the freedom to create more complex designs than they may be able to do directly onto the wall.

WHAT DO YOU THINK?

Wheatpaste posters can be removed using a scraper, soap, and water. Is illegal wheatpasting vandalism? It costs money to employ people to clean wheatpaste posters off the walls.

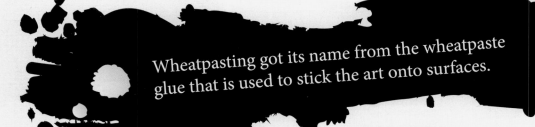

Wheatpasting got its name from the wheatpaste glue that is used to stick the art onto surfaces.

Wheatpasting started out as a way for small companies to promote themselves. The advertising was often done illegally. Street artists then started wheatpasting, as it was a good way of quickly getting their work to a large audience.

A face wheatpasted onto a trash can by the German Berlin-based street artist group "Mentalgassi."

LOST

Treefort Monster!
7'2" 560 lbs, Brown fur, Stone head.
Last seen at Boise150 Sesqui-Shop.

Event organizers often use wheatpaste posters as a way of advertising their event. This "Lost" poster is good at getting people's attention. The tear-off strips along the bottom advertize a music festival.

Sticker Bombing

Stickers are used by some street artists to create images or messages. Some artists hand draw art onto blank stickers. Others design and print hundreds of stickers using home computers and printers, or even pay to print them at a print shop.

Sticker artists have different reasons behind why they create their stickers. Some artists want to make people smile. Some want to get people thinking. Other sticker artists just want to get their art in as many places as possible. Sticker artists will often swap batches of stickers with people in other areas or other countries. This way, their work is spread as far as possible.

This wheatpaste piece, named BatBond, is by Montreal street artist Stikki Peaches. Originally, the words "What if art ruled the world?" were written on his body. The words are now covered in other people's stickers! You can see smaller stickers of BatBond on the art, too.

It is expensive and time-consuming to remove stickers. Placing stickers on other people's property is **vandalism**. Vandalism is when someone deliberately damages public or private property.

This sticker-bombed trashcan will look ugly when the stickers fade and peel.

Street artist Shepard Fairey created thousands of "André the Giant" stickers. He wanted to see how quickly the image became recognized.

ANDRE THE GIANT HAS A POSSE 7'4" 520LB

The way the word "art" is placed on this stop sign could be seen as clever, or dangerous. The stop sign is there to make people stop, not start!

STOP / START

WHAT DO YOU THINK?

Do you think sticking stickers in public places is art? Does it matter what the sticker says, or what it is a picture of? Does it matter where it is stuck?

Ben Wilson, Gum Artist!

Artist Ben Wilson creates tiny works of art by painting chewing gum that is stuck to the sidewalk! Wilson is based in London, England and has painted many thousands of pieces of gum, in his local area, and also worldwide.

Actual size!

It takes Wilson around three hours to produce each piece. First he finds some spat-out gum on the sidewalk and heats it with a blowtorch. He covers it with lacquer followed by two coats of paint. Once the base layer has dried, he paints the design. Then he lacquers over the finished painting and heats it up again. Now the gum is waterproof and can be walked on.

Ben Wilson at work painting a piece of gum.

WHAT DO YOU THINK?

Ben has been arrested for painting gum. He is not damaging property, just painting trash. Do you think what he does is wrong? Dropping gum is littering, so dropping it is wrong. But what about painting it?

Ben Wilson usually signs his tiny gum paintings with either "B.W." or "chewing gum man" if there's room!

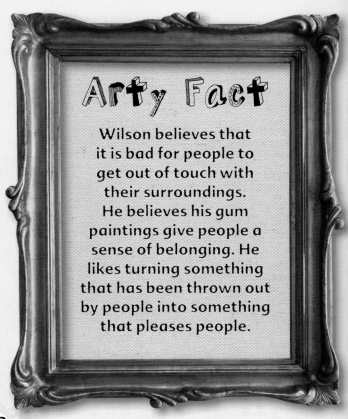

While Wilson is working on a painting, people come up to him and ask him to paint a piece of gum for them. He doesn't take any money for doing it. His biggest regret was losing two books containing a few hundred requests from people. The requests make the gum very personal to the area where they are painted. The gum pictures connect the local people to their area in a fun way. It's exciting to have your name painted for everyone to see on the sidewalk where you live!

Arty Fact

Wilson believes that it is bad for people to get out of touch with their surroundings. He believes his gum paintings give people a sense of belonging. He likes turning something that has been thrown out by people into something that pleases people.

Lovelocks

Lovelocks are an unusual form of lock on art. It is a romantic tradition in some places for a couple to write their names onto a padlock, fasten it onto railings or a bridge and throw away the key. The tradition is meant to symbolize unbreakable love.

While this seems a harmless, romantic thing to do, many bridges are struggling under the weight of these padlocks! The padlocks can damage the structure they are padlocked to, and are costly to remove. To discourage people from using bridge railings, some local authorities build iron trees for the lovelocks to go on instead!

WHAT DO YOU THINK?

Are lovelocks art? One padlock might not be considered art. What about when there are thousands of them, all symbolizing love? Has it become a sculpture? The padlocks certainly express strong feelings.

Love padlocks in France on the Pont des Arts, Paris. The weight of the locks on this footbridge over the river Seine weigh around 93 metric tons! In June 2014, part of the bridge collapsed under the weight.

Arty Fact

At the N Seoul Tower in South Korea, there are key bins for couples to put the key in once they have locked their padlock to the railings. Couples used to throw the key from the top of the tower. This was dangerous. A key hitting a passerby after falling hundreds of feet (meters) through the air can hurt!

A key bin at the N Seoul Tower, South Korea.

Purpose-built trees have been put on a bridge across a canal in Moscow, Russia. Brides and grooms often have their photograph taken attaching their padlock to a tree.

Guerrilla Gardening

Guerrilla gardeners turn disused space into gardens! The gardeners are not legally allowed to do it. Because they are creating gardens on land that is not being cared for, people don't usually mind.

The word "guerrilla" describes a person who is not in the military who helps to fight a war. Some guerrilla gardeners garden as a form of protest. They want to reclaim land that is being neglected or misused. Others simply want to grow things and make the area more appealing.

Sunflowers are often used by guerrilla gardeners to brighten up a roadside.

Guerrilla gardeners often grow food crops. These tomato and basil plants are planted in an old, dumped drawer at this neglected site.

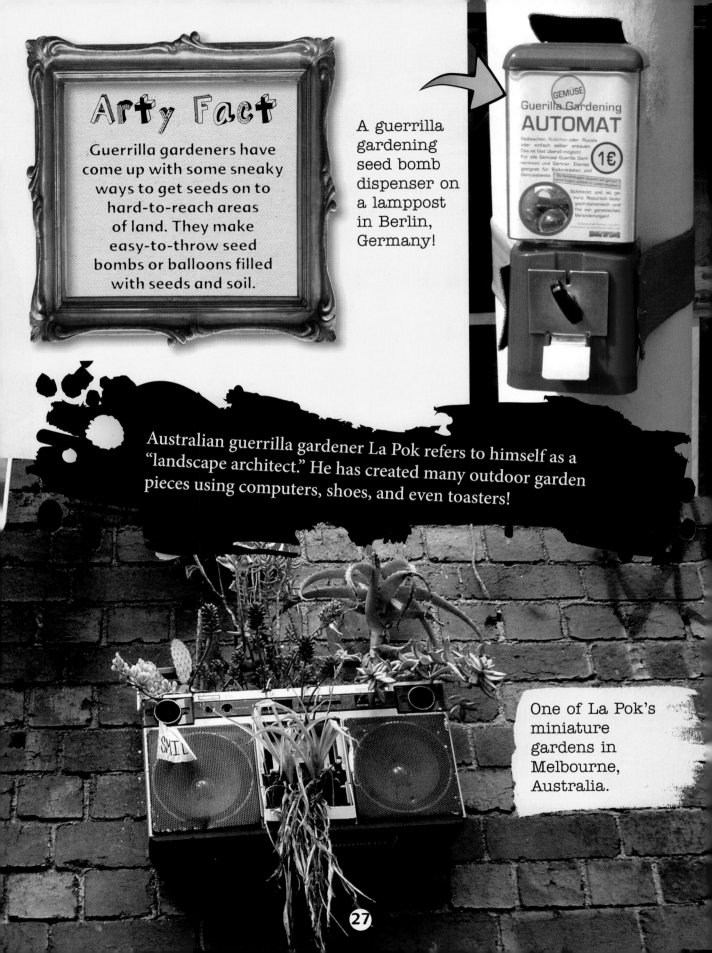

Arty Fact

Guerrilla gardeners have come up with some sneaky ways to get seeds on to hard-to-reach areas of land. They make easy-to-throw seed bombs or balloons filled with seeds and soil.

A guerrilla gardening seed bomb dispenser on a lamppost in Berlin, Germany!

GEMÜSE
Guerilla Gardening
AUTOMAT
Radieschen, Rübchen oder Rucola oder einfach selber anbauen. Das ist fast überall möglich! Für alle Gemüse Guerilla Gärtnerinnen und Gärtner. Ebenso geeignet für Balkonkästen und Gemüsebeete. Die Samenkugeln recycelt wir gemusst – ihren Kugeln gerben im Leben abgeben.
Schmeckt und ist gesund. Natürlich biologisch-dynamisch und frei von genetischen Veränderungen!

1€

Australian guerrilla gardener La Pok refers to himself as a "landscape architect." He has created many outdoor garden pieces using computers, shoes, and even toasters!

One of La Pok's miniature gardens in Melbourne, Australia.

Is Urban Street Art Art?

Have you made up your mind? Is urban street art art? To help you, have a look at some of these arguments "for" and "against."

Urban Street Art IS Art

- If the artists call it art, it must be art
- Street art can contain important or interesting political messages
- It can help improve the look of an area
- If artists are expressing themselves it must be art
- Museums and galleries exhibit some street art
- Street art attracts tourists from around the world
- Street art can be very beautiful and skillful

Urban Street Art ISN'T Art

- Some forms of street art aren't very skillful, such as guerrilla gardening
- Street art can make an area look ugly
- It costs money to clean away some street art, such as wheatpaste posters
- Why should it be up to street artists to decide what our streets look like?
- Some street art is vandalism and illegal
- If street art was artistic why has it been made illegal?

Street art, such as this ghost bike, can make you stop and think. This ghost bike may even save a life by making motorists more careful.

Street art allows artists to reach a much larger audience than exhibiting at art galleries would.

Some forms of street art could make good exhibits in an art gallery. Other types really only make sense in a street environment. If you put a drawer with some tomato plants in an art gallery, it would not have the same impact as it does in an area of wasteland. Street art really only makes sense on the street.

WHAT DO YOU THINK?

If you are not sure, that's OK. Perhaps some street art could be called art and some couldn't? Which artists or types of street art do you think could be called art?

Glossary

advertisements
Acts or processes of advertising.

anonymous
Not named or identified.

consumerism
The belief that it is good for people to spend a lot of money on goods and services.

distorted
Twisted out of a natural, normal, or original shape or condition.

graffiti
Usually unlawful writing or drawing on a public surface.

illegal
Against the law.

installation
A work of art consisting of different components shown in a large space.

laser
A device that uses the natural vibrations of atoms to make a narrow beam of light.

LEDs
Electronic devices that give off light when electricity is applied.

Madonna
The mother of Jesus Christ.

optical illusion
Something that deceives the eye by appearing to be other than it is.

political
Involving, concerned with, or accused of acts against a government or political system.

projectors
Machines for projecting an image or pictures upon a surface

studio
The working place of an artist.

vandalism
Intentional destruction or damage to property.

wavelength
An electromagnetic wave used to send signals through the air without using wires.

For More Information

Books

Gogerly, Liz. *Graffiti Culture*. Minneapolis, MN: Lerner, 2012.

Greve, Tom. *A Look at Urban Art*. Vero Beach, FL:
Rourke Publishing Group, 2013.

Sutherland, Adam. *Street Art*. Minneapolis, MN: Lerner, 2012.

Websites

Tate Gallery
http://kids.tate.org.uk/games/street-art/
Great website designed for kids with an interest in art. Interactive site
where you can create your own graffiti.

Publisher's note to educators and parents:
Our editors have carefully reviewed these websites
to ensure that they are suitable for students. Many
websites change frequently, however, and we cannot
guarantee that a site's future contents will continue
to meet our high standards of quality and educational
value. Be advised that students should be closely
supervised whenever they access the Internet.

Index

A
advertise 8, 9, 16, 19

B
Banksy 12, 13
Brandalism 9

E
English, Ron 8, 9

F
Fairey, Shepard 13, 21
Fekner, John 5

G
ghost bikes 15, 29
graffiti 4, 11
guerrilla gardening 4, 26–29

I
Indiana, Scott Wayne 15

K
Knit the City 7

L
La Pok 27
lasers 11
LEDs 10, 11
lock ons 14, 15, 24, 25
lovelocks 24, 25

M
Metalgassi 19

S
sidewalk art 16, 17
stickers 20, 21
Stikki Peaches 20
subvertising 8, 9

T
Tejn 14

V
vandalism 18, 21, 28

W
wheatpasting 18–20, 28
White Nights 10
Wilson, Ben 22, 23

Y
yarn bombing 5–7